The Celebrated Jumping Frog of Calaveras County

A Humorous Tall Tale of Trickery, Gambling & the Wild Charm of the American West

A Modern Translation
Adapted for the Contemporary Reader

Mark Twain

Translated by Tim Zengerink

Table of Contents

Preface Message to the Reader 1

Introduction 2

The Celebrated Jumping Frog of Calaveras
        County 10

Thank You For Reading 19

Preface
Message to the Reader

Rebuilding the Greatest Library in Human History

Thousands of years ago, the Library of Alexandria was the heart of global knowledge — a sanctuary where the wisdom of every known civilization was gathered and shared freely.

And then, it was lost.

Now, we're rebuilding it — and you are invited to join us.

At the Library of Alexandria, we've set out to make every book available to every person on Earth — not just in print, but in every language, every format, and for every reader.

Here's how we do it:

- **Deluxe Print Editions at True Printing Cost** - Order any book as a high-quality paperback, elegant hardcover, or stunning boxset — and only pay what it costs to print. No markups. No middlemen.
- **Unlimited Access to the Greatest Works** - Enjoy thousands of timeless classics — from Plato to Shakespeare to Tolstoy — in beautiful, modern eBook and audiobook editions. Read and listen without limits — for every reader, everywhere.
- **Modern Translations for Every Language & Dialect** - We're reimagining the classics in clear, accessible language — and translating them into every dialect imaginable. Everyone deserves to understand humanity's greatest ideas.

When you visit **LibraryofAlexandria.com**, you're not just accessing books — you're joining a global movement to restore, preserve, and share the wisdom of civilization.

Join us today at LibraryofAlexandria.com

Together, we'll ensure the light of human wisdom never fades again.

With gratitude,

The Modern Library of Alexandria Team

Visit:
www.libraryofalexandria.com
Or scan the code below:

Introduction

The Birth of an American Literary Voice

There are certain works of literature that seem to carry with them the essence of a nation's character—its humor, its contradictions, its sense of possibility and its rough-hewn charm. Mark Twain's *The Celebrated Jumping Frog of Calaveras County* is such a work. First published in 1865 in the New York Saturday Press, this seemingly simple story about a boastful gambler and his extraordinary frog brought its author, Samuel Langhorne Clemens—better known by his pen name, Mark Twain—his first taste of national fame. Yet the story is more than a humorous anecdote or a clever piece of frontier folklore. It is a testament to the American spirit of improvisation, a reflection of the rugged and eccentric character of the West, and a foundational text in the evolution of American literary humor.

This introduction aims to provide the reader with a comprehensive appreciation of Twain's tale, preparing them to experience not just the laughter it provokes but also the cultural and literary significance it holds. To achieve this, we will delve deeply into the historical context of the story, explore its narrative techniques and themes, and consider its role in shaping Mark Twain's career and, by extension, the trajectory of American literature. For those who might view *The Celebrated Jumping Frog of Calaveras County* as "just" a tall tale, this exploration will reveal that beneath the comic surface lies a carefully constructed narrative that captures the vernacular voice, social dynamics, and playful irreverence that would become Twain's trademarks.

The story revolves around an unnamed narrator who, at the request of a friend, visits Simon Wheeler to inquire about an old acquaintance. Wheeler responds by spinning an elaborate and often absurd tale about Jim Smiley, a compulsive gambler with a knack for betting on anything and everything—from horse races to dog fights to, most famously, the jumping abilities of a frog named Dan'l Webster. What begins as a simple anecdote quickly transforms into a rollicking portrait of frontier life, full of exaggerated characters, sharp wit, and a subtle mockery of both the storyteller and the listener.

The genius of this story lies not in its plot, which is simple and linear, but in its execution. Twain employs the narrative voice of Simon Wheeler—a slow-talking, seemingly naïve storyteller—whose rustic charm and colloquial phrasing bring the frontier world to life. The humor emerges from the contrast between Wheeler's deadpan delivery and the outrageous content of his tale, as well as from Twain's skillful use of understatement, repetition, and local dialect. It is a humor that feels organic, springing from character and circumstance rather than from forced punchlines.

But to truly appreciate *The Celebrated Jumping Frog of Calaveras County*, it is essential to understand the literary and cultural environment in which Twain was writing. The mid-19th century was a period of rapid expansion and transformation in the United States. The Gold Rush of 1849 had drawn countless fortune-seekers westward, creating a landscape of both chaos and opportunity. California, with its saloons, mining camps, and transient populations, became a breeding ground for tall tales and exaggerated storytelling. Oral humor flourished in these settings, as people gathered around campfires or in dimly lit taverns to share stories that blended fact and fiction with equal gusto. Twain, who had spent time working as a reporter in California and Nevada, absorbed this oral tradition and transformed it into literary art.

This story marked a turning point in Twain's life. Before its publication, he had worked various jobs—printer's apprentice, steamboat pilot, journalist—without achieving lasting recognition. The success of "The Jumping Frog" launched his career as a humorist and gave him a platform to refine the narrative voice that would later power classics like The Adventures of Tom Sawyer and Adventures of Huckleberry Finn. In many ways, this story serves as a blueprint for Twain's later works, showcasing his ability to elevate the everyday speech of ordinary people into something both comically exaggerated and artistically enduring.

Humor, Trickery, and the Art of the Tall Tale

At its core, *The Celebrated Jumping Frog of Calaveras County* is a story about trickery—both the tricks played by the characters on one another and the narrative tricks Twain plays on the reader. Jim Smiley, the hapless gambler, is a man of endless curiosity and compulsive risk-taking. He will bet on anything that moves—or even on things that don't. His legendary frog, Dan'l Webster, is the centerpiece of his betting schemes, trained to jump higher and farther than any other frog in Calaveras County. But Smiley's overconfidence proves to be his downfall when a sly stranger fills Dan'l Webster with buckshot, ensuring that the frog is too heavy to jump. Smiley loses his bet and, with it, his pride.

This scenario encapsulates a central theme of the story: the tension between cleverness and gullibility. Smiley is both the trickster and the tricked, a man whose ingenuity is undone by his own obsession with gambling. Twain uses this dynamic to poke fun at human nature, illustrating how our strengths—when taken to excess—can become weaknesses. The story suggests that even the most cunning individuals can be outwitted by those who are just as cunning, or perhaps by those who seem simple but are quietly observant.

The humor of the story is multilayered. On the surface, it is the absurdity of the situations—the idea of a man obsessively training a frog to jump, or betting on which bird will fly off a fence post first—that elicits laughter. But on a deeper level, the humor arises from Twain's mastery of voice and timing. Simon Wheeler's narrative style is deliberately slow and rambling, filled with digressions and redundant details that both frustrate and amuse the reader. The contrast between Wheeler's earnest delivery and the ridiculousness of his content creates a comedic tension that is quintessentially Twain.

Furthermore, Twain's use of dialect and colloquial speech gives the story an authenticity that was groundbreaking for its time. In an era when American literature was often dominated by formal and European-influenced styles, Twain's decision to capture the rhythms of everyday American speech was both bold and revolutionary. He demonstrated that humor and artistry could be found not in elevated language, but in the vernacular of ordinary people. This approach not only set him apart from his contemporaries but also paved the way for future generations of American writers.

The story also plays with the concept of the unreliable narrator. The unnamed frame narrator, who is sent to interview Wheeler, is clearly skeptical of the tale he is being told. He becomes both a participant and a victim of Wheeler's rambling, unable to extract himself from the story even as he recognizes its absurdity. In this way, Twain invites the reader to share in the narrator's frustration and amusement, creating a layered narrative structure that is as much about the act of storytelling as it is about the story itself.

Finally, *The Celebrated Jumping Frog of Calaveras County* exemplifies the tradition of the tall tale, a uniquely American form of storytelling that thrives on exaggeration, irony, and playful deception. Like the best tall tales, Twain's story blurs the line between truth and fiction, encouraging readers to suspend disbelief while simultaneously winking at them through its absurdity. It is a narrative that revels in its own artifice, reminding us that stories are as much about the way they are told as about what they contain.

Twain's Legacy and the Reader's Journey

Reading *The Celebrated Jumping Frog of Calaveras County* today is not just an encounter with a humorous story—it is a chance to witness the birth of a literary giant. Mark Twain would go on to become one of America's greatest writers, celebrated for his wit, social commentary, and keen understanding of human nature. But this story, with its humble beginnings and playful tone, laid the foundation for everything that followed. It was here that Twain first demonstrated his ability to blend humor with insight, to turn the quirks of everyday life into enduring art.

For modern readers, the story offers both entertainment and a window into the cultural landscape of 19th-century America. It captures the spirit of a time when the West was still wild, when communities were built on equal parts hard labor and tall tales, and when humor served as both a form of entertainment and a way of coping with the hardships of frontier life. The characters—though exaggerated—reflect real human tendencies: the desire to outwit others, the thrill of competition, the stubborn belief in one's own cleverness.

To fully appreciate the story, readers should pay close attention to Twain's language. Notice the cadence of Wheeler's speech, the way he lingers on details that seem trivial but build the atmosphere of the tale. Observe the narrator's shifting reactions, from polite interest to barely concealed impatience. And consider the story's ending, which leaves us with both laughter and a lingering sense of the absurdity of human endeavors.

Moreover, this story is best enjoyed with a willingness to read between the lines. While it may appear lighthearted, Twain's humor often carries a sharper edge. He subtly mocks the pretensions of those who believe they are clever, the gullibility of those who fall for obvious tricks, and even the process of storytelling itself. In this sense, *The Celebrated Jumping Frog of Calaveras County* is both a celebration of humor and a gentle critique of the ways we amuse ourselves.

In conclusion, as you embark on this reading journey, consider this story not just as an isolated piece of entertainment but as a cornerstone of American literary history. It is a reminder that great art can emerge from the simplest of premises, that humor can be as profound as tragedy, and that the voice of one storyteller—armed with nothing more than wit and observation—can resonate across centuries.

Enjoy this tale for its humor, its craft, and its place in the grand tapestry of American storytelling. Let yourself laugh, let yourself marvel, and above all, let yourself be reminded of the timeless joy of a well-told tale.

The Celebrated Jumping Frog of Calaveras County

In compliance with the request of a friend of mine, who wrote me from the East, I called on good-natured, garrulous old Simon Wheeler, and inquired after my friend's friend, Leonidas W. Smiley, as requested to do, and I hereunto append the result. I have a lurking suspicion that Leonidas W. Smiley is a myth that my friend never knew such a personage; and that he only conjectured that if I asked old Wheeler about him, it would remind him of his infamous Jim Smiley, and he would go to work and bore me to death with some exasperating reminiscence of him as long and as tedious as it should be useless to me. If that was the design, it succeeded.

I found Simon Wheeler dozing comfortably by the bar-room stove of the dilapidated tavern in the decayed mining camp of Angel's, and I noticed that he was fat and bald-headed, and had an expression of winning gentleness and simplicity upon his tranquil countenance. He roused up, and gave me good day. I told him that a friend of mine had commissioned me to make some inquiries about a cherished companion of his boyhood named Leonidas W. Smiley—Rev. Leonidas W. Smiley, a young minister of the Gospel, who he had heard was at one time resident of Angel's Camp. I added that if Mr. Wheeler could tell me anything about this Rev. Leonidas W. Smiley, I would feel under many obligations to him.

Simon Wheeler backed me into a corner and blockaded me there with his chair, and then sat down and reeled off the monotonous narrative which follows this paragraph. He never smiled, he never frowned, he never changed his voice from the gentle flowing key to which he tuned his initial sentence, he never betrayed the slightest suspicion of enthusiasm; but all through the interminable narrative there ran a vein of impressive earnestness and sincerity, which showed me plainly that, so far from his imagining that there was anything ridiculous or funny about his story, he regarded it as a really important matter, and admired its two heroes as men of transcendent genius in 'finesse.' I let him go on in his own way, and never interrupted him once.

"Rev. Leonidas W. H'm, Reverend Le—well, there was a feller here, once by the name of Jim Smiley, in the winter of '49—or maybe it was the spring of '50—I don't recollect exactly, somehow, though what makes me think it was one or the other is because I remember the big flume warn't finished when he first come to the camp; but anyway, he was the curiousest man about always betting on anything that turned up you ever see, if he could get anybody to bet on the other side; and if he couldn't he'd change sides. Any way that suited the other man would suit him any way just so's he got a bet, he was satisfied. But still he was lucky, uncommon lucky; he most always come out winner. He was always ready and laying for a chance; there couldn't be no solit'ry thing mentioned but that feller'd offer to bet on it, and take any side you please, as I was just telling you.

If there was a horse-race, you'd find him flush or you'd find him busted at the end of it; if there was a dog-fight, he'd bet on it; if there was a cat-fight, he'd bet on it; if there was a chicken-fight, he'd bet on it; why, if there was two birds setting on a fence, he would bet you which one would fly first; or if there was a camp-meeting, he would be there reg'lar to bet on Parson Walker, which he judged to be the best exhorter about here, and so he was too, and a good man. If he even see a straddle-bug start to go anywheres, he would bet you how long it would take him to get to—to wherever he was going to, and if you took him up, he would foller that straddle-bug to Mexico but what he would find out where he was bound for and how long he was on the road. Lots of the boys here has seen that Smiley, and can tell you about him. Why, it never made no difference to him— he'd bet on any thing—the dangdest feller. Parson Walker's wife laid very sick once, for a good while, and it seemed as if they warn't going to save her; but one morning he come in, and Smiley up and asked him how she was, and he said she was considerable better—thank the Lord for his inf'nite mercy—and coming on so smart that with the blessing of Prov'dence she'd get well yet; and Smiley, before he thought, says, 'Well, I'll resk two-and-a-half she don't anyway.'

"Thish-yer Smiley had a mare—the boys called her the fifteen-minute nag, but that was only in fun, you know, because of course she was faster than that—and he used to win money on that horse, for all she was so slow and always had the asthma, or the distemper, or the consumption, or something of that kind. They used to give her two or three hundred yards' start, and then pass her under way; but always at the fag end of the race she get excited and desperate like, and come cavorting and straddling up, and scattering her legs around limber, sometimes in the air, and sometimes out to one side among the fences, and kicking up m-o-r-e dust and raising m-o-r-e racket with her coughing and sneezing and blowing her nose—and always fetch up at the stand just about a neck ahead, as near as you could cipher it down.

"And he had a little small bull-pup, that to look at him you'd think he warn't worth a cent but to set around and look ornery and lay for a chance to steal something. But as soon as money was up on him he was a different dog; his under-jaw'd begin to stick out like the fo'castle of a steamboat, and his teeth would uncover and shine like the furnaces. And a dog might tackle him and bully-rag him, and bite him, and throw him over his shoulder two or three times, and Andrew Jackson—which was the name of the pup—Andrew Jackson would never let on but what he was satisfied, and hadn't expected nothing else—and the bets being doubled and doubled on the other side all the time, till the money was all up; and then all of a sudden he would grab that other dog jest by the j'int of his hind leg and freeze to it—not chaw, you understand, but only just grip and hang on till they throwed up the sponge, if it was a year. Smiley always come out winner on that pup, till he harnessed a dog once that didn't have no hind legs, because they'd been sawed off in a circular saw, and when the thing had gone along far enough, and the money was all up, and he come to make a snatch for his pet holt, he see in a minute how he'd been imposed on, and how the other dog had him in the door, so to speak, and he 'peared surprised, and then he looked sorter discouraged-like and didn't try no more to win the fight, and so he got shucked out bad. He give Smiley a look, as much as to say his heart was broke, and it was his fault, for putting up a dog that hadn't no hind legs for him to take holt of, which was his main dependence in a fight, and then he limped off a piece and laid down and died. It was a good pup, was that Andrew Jackson, and would have made a name for hisself if he'd lived, for the stuff was in him and he had genius—I know it, because he hadn't no opportunities to speak of, and it don't stand to reason that a dog could make such a fight as he could under them circumstances if he hadn't no talent. It always makes me feel sorry when I think of that last fight of his'n, and the way it turned out.

"Well, thish-yer Smiley had rat-tarriers, and chicken cocks, and tomcats and all them kind of things, till you couldn't rest, and you couldn't fetch nothing for him to bet on but he'd match you. He ketched a frog one day, and took him home, and said he cal'lated to educate him; and so he never done nothing for three months but set in his back yard and learn that frog to jump. And you bet you he did learn him, too. He'd give him a little punch behind, and the next minute you'd see that frog whirling in the air like a doughnut—see him turn one summerset, or maybe a couple, if he got a good start, and come down flat-footed and all right, like a cat. He got him up so in the matter of ketching flies, and kep' him in practice so constant, that he'd nail a fly every time as fur as he could see him. Smiley said all a frog wanted was education, and he could do 'most anything—and I believe him. Why, I've seen him set Dan'l Webster down here on this floor—Dan'l Webster was the name of the frog—and sing out, 'Flies, Dan'l, flies!' and quicker'n you could wink he'd spring straight up and snake a fly off'n the counter there, and flop down on the floor ag'in as solid as a gob of mud, and fall to scratching the side of his head with his hind foot as indifferent as if he hadn't no idea he'd been doin' any more'n any frog might do. You never see a frog so modest and straightfor'ard as he was, for all he was so gifted. And when it come to fair and square jumping on a dead level, he could get over more ground at one straddle than any animal of his breed you ever see. Jumping on a dead level was his strong suit, you understand; and when it come to that, Smiley would ante up money on him as long as he had a red. Smiley was monstrous proud of his frog, and well he might be, for fellers that had traveled and been everywheres all said he laid over any frog that ever they see.

"Well, Smiley kep' the beast in a little lattice box, and he used to fetch him down-town sometimes and lay for a bet. One day a feller—a stranger in the camp, he was—come acrost him with his box, and says:

"'What might it be that you've got in the box?'

"And Smiley says, sorter indifferent-like, 'It might be a parrot, or it might be a canary, maybe, but it ain't—it's only just a frog.'

"And the feller took it, and looked at it careful, and turned it round this way and that, and says, 'H'm—so 'tis. Well, what's HE good for.

"'Well,' Smiley says, easy and careless, 'he's good enough for one thing, I should judge—he can outjump any frog in Calaveras County.

"The feller took the box again, and took another long, particular look, and give it back to Smiley, and says, very deliberate, 'Well,' he says, 'I don't see no p'ints about that frog that's any better'n any other frog.'

"'Maybe you don't,' Smiley says. 'Maybe you understand frogs and maybe you don't understand 'em; maybe you've had experience, and maybe you ain't only a amature, as it were. Anyways, I've got my opinion, and I'll resk forty dollars thet he can outjump any frog in Calaveras County.'

"And the feller studied a minute, and then says, kinder sad-like, 'Well, I'm only a stranger here, and I ain't got no frog; but if I had a frog, I'd bet you.

"And then Smiley says, 'That's all right—that's all right if you'll hold my box a minute, I'll go and get you a frog.' And so the feller took the box, and put up his forty dollars along with Smiley's, and set down to wait.

"So he set there a good while thinking and thinking to himself and then he got the frog out and prized his mouth open and took a teaspoon and filled him full of quail-shot—filled him pretty near up to his chin—and set him on the floor. Smiley he went to the swamp and slopped around in the mud for a long time, and finally he ketched a frog, and fetched him in, and give him to this feller and says:

"'Now, if you're ready, set him alongside of Dan'l, with his fore paws just even with Dan'l's, and I'll give the word.' Then he says, One-two-three—git' and him and the feller touches up the frogs from behind, and the new frog hopped off lively but Dan'l give a heave, and hysted up his shoulders—so—like a Frenchman, but it warn't no use—he couldn't budge; he was planted as solid as a church, and he couldn't no more stir than if he was anchored out. Smiley was a good deal surprised, and he was disgusted too, but he didn't have no idea what the matter was of course.

"The feller took the money and started away; and when he was going out at the door, he sorter jerked his thumb over his shoulder—so—at Dan'l, and says again, very deliberate, 'Well,' he says, 'I don't see no p'ints about that frog that's any better'n any other frog.'

"Smiley he stood scratching his head and looking down at Dan'l a long time, and at last he says, 'I do wonder what in the nation that frog throw'd off for—I wonder if there ain't something the matter with him—he 'pears to look mighty baggy, somehow.' And he ketched Dan'l by the nap of the neck, and hefted him, and says, 'Why blame my cats if he don't weigh five pound!' and turned him upside down and he belched out a double handful of shot. And then he see how it was, and he was the maddest man—he set the frog down and took out after that feller, but he never ketched him. And—"

[Here Simon Wheeler heard his name called from the front yard, and got up to see what was wanted.] And turning to me as he moved away, he said: "Just set where you are, stranger, and rest easy—I ain't going to be gone a second."

But, by your leave, I did not think that a continuation of the history of the enterprising vagabond Jim Smiley would be likely to afford me much information concerning the Rev. Leonidas W. Smiley, and so I started away.

At the door I met the sociable Wheeler returning, and he buttonholed me and recommenced:

"Well, thish-yer Smiley had a yaller one-eyed cow that didn't have no tail, only just a short stump like a bannanner, and—"

However, lacking both time and inclination, I did not wait to hear about the afflicted cow, but took my leave.

Thank You For Reading

You've Just Read a Piece of the Greatest Library Ever Rebuilt

Thank you for reading.

This book is one of thousands we're restoring, reimagining, and translating as part of the **Modern Library of Alexandria** — a global movement to preserve and share humanity's most important ideas.

What was once lost to fire and time is now rising again — not just as memory, but as living, breathing knowledge, freely accessible to all.

What You Can Do Next:

- **Keep Reading.**

  Discover more legendary works — in beautiful print, audiobook, or digital form — at LibraryofAlexandria.com.

- **Build Your Own Library.**

  Every title is available as a paperback, hardcover, or collectible boxset — at true printing cost. Craft a personal library worthy of display.

- **Spread the Light.**

  Share this book. Tell others about the movement. Help us translate every timeless work into every language, so no reader is ever left behind.

By finishing this book, you've already taken part in something extraordinary.

Join us at LibraryofAlexandria.com

Together, we're rebuilding the greatest library the world has ever known.

With appreciation,

The Modern Library of Alexandria Team

Visit:
www.libraryofalexandria.com
Or scan the code below:

www.ingramcontent.com/pod-product-compliance
Lightning Source LLC
Chambersburg PA
CBHW010335040726
47494CB00027BB/2375